Empty Dresses

Empty Dresses

Julie Chevalier

PUNCHER & WATTMANN

First published in 2023
Published by Puncher and Wattmann
PO Box 279
Waratah NSW 2298

https://www.puncherandwattmann.com
web@puncherandwattmann.com

ISBN   9781922571557

Cover design by Gary Pedler (Scampe Consulting) and David Musgrave
Artwork by Julie Chevalier
Typesetting by Morgan Arnett
Printed by Lightning Source International

A catalogue record for this work is available from the National Library of Australia

NATIONAL
LIBRARY
OF AUSTRALIA

Contents

1

2

dedicated to my wonderful family
with much love

Simon, Rilka, Indigo, Ariel, Mars and Rome
Anna, Aran, Oscar, Sasha and Til

Artemisia Gentileschi Plays Wordle

blank paper	white paper
study hands	watch faces
sepia skill	paint model
plays light	draws music
roman anger	naked spite
rowdy cheat	party prank
thick beard	block mouth

knees force thigh apart

girl's irate tutor tassi

rapes rival

tough holds   fight bleed

"At the time they said Agostino attacked me I was having my period and therefore I am not able to say certainly to your Lordship whether my vagina bled because of what Agostino did because I did not know much about how these things happen; but it is true that it seemed to me that the blood was redder than usual."

judge knows hymen broke

black paint	heavy wings
libel trial	court brutal
adult rebel	mercy mercy

Susannah and the Elders

elder leech   seedy touch

three males   tower above

young woman   youth shame

rapes begin   genre scene

Judith and Holofernes

fluid gowns   laced tight

devil shows angel flesh

ivory light   drink drunk

angry blade   strong knife

timid tough   wreck myths

grand wield   strike again

sever cords   blood spurts

agony waits   death stops

who would ravish a tree

after Bernini's sculpture, *Apollo and Daphne*, Galleria Borghese, Rome

bernini chose cold carrara marble for my warm skin
      marble?

                        i was   serious   aloof

        after cupid's double mischief with arrows —
        mischief?   let's call it toxic masculinity —
                i became apollo's magnet

    if apollo were as sensitive
    as he was beautiful
    i might have desired him
    but i was repulsed

          it is true
          cupid & apollo wrecked my life

                  apollo called me ravishing
                i drowned in his compliments
              no one had called me pretty
         & i had seen reflections in the river

    i turned from his grabbing & grasping
    reached for the sky
    his torso twisted me
    twisted around me
    his lust bound me to earth

        my witness   the galleria borghese   i swear

stop   let go of me fuckwit
let   me   go
first i screamed then i whimpered
i can't breathe   damn you
i   fucking   can   not   breathe ﹏

i beseeched my river god father for help

he turned me into a tree

turned me wooden

clothed me in laurel

i welcomed each change   each leaf

but apollo's hands searched & beseeched

the places he touched turned into bark
my toes dug into earth
leaves grew from my hands

i hear gallery visitors gossiping
apollo blamed cupid's arrow
he claimed she flirted   led him on
tempted him with nakedness
he pleaded innocence

can you believe it?
that i giggled when he tickled?
i the solemn one?

empty dresses

after artwork by Anselm Kiefer

lilith's daughters

after (*Liliths Töchter*) 1991

sepia night falls on ashen children
hours extend from mother's dress
only hours remain to protect five daughters
she wraps them in her cloak
imagines her arms are wings

the crunch of wheels on snow
the nightcart man collecting plague corpses
shovels stuttering on frozen ground

from the mother's sleeves hang leaden planes
toys offering hope rather than flight
the lead refuses to lift
the daughters turn from their mother   afraid
even of her   they are afraid

the eldest's yellow scarf not golden enough
not potent enough   to ward off contagion
the middle child clutches strands of long dark hair
herbs & chants not strong enough to stem the pandemic

lacking immunity   no one's will is strong enough
no one's arms are long enough
while snow gently falls   bless
the empty dresses adrift
if found, deliver the vulnerable

fill your pockets with stones,
the river beckons the daughters
a celestial map hangs from mother's neck
an anchor hanging from snakeskin

but i am not a shaman   & kiefer says
the words he scratches on paintings
are meant to confuse   so forget lilith
forget clawed succubae
we are all daughters

quotidian

after *Die Argonauten*, 1990

a one prop plane with a dip in its spine
scuds the gritty floor —
        this plane made of lead must be the argo

twisted vapour trails
fragile as overcooked linguine
        hang from wings & tail

why is the impotent plane dragging
cut outs on oversized hangers?
        two dimensional clothes   paint spotted

dresses   tee shirts   the smocks of children
& on the studio floor   footprints
        a battered suitcase   buckets of paint

some clothes-kites detach
escape responsibilities

baby's sleeve will never
touch mummy's empty sleeve

the order of the angels

after Die Ordnung der Engel, 2000

constellation names whirl clockwise
an infinity of linen sweeps a firmament
a galaxy of dresses   bodices   smocks
clothes: faded   passionless   sapped of energy
circle with the clunking of a tired
merry-go-round in a museum
a cyclone of homeless angels unable to rest
unable to sleep   the larger clothes
receding   preparing to bed down
while children play games outside
the sleeves of one shift directing hereafter traffic
go back   wrong way
too many regrets   too many rules
the shadow of the marimekko dress i wore
beneath a camphor laurel fifty years ago
the arms that wrapped my baby
now outstretched
i release abandoned layettes
set the babies & grandbabies free
garments unfettered as memories

Black Cockatoo Feather Fan

David Daymirrinu Malagi, c1984, Yolnu Foundation, East Arnhem Land,
The Chau Chak Wing Museum, Sydney
feathers, beeswax, wood

eight chunky black & orange feathers
not like black cockatoos on the central coast   ours don't have orange
black & yellow in the illawarra   wylah wylah   so distinctive pre-schoolers
    recognise their cry
same in moore park
the quills are stuck in something tarry
it says beeswax   but dark for beeswax
discoloured   from age perhaps
narrows to the width of one quill   wooden
strikingly graphic   blackorangeblack   stark simple bands   i always tell my
design students   keep it simple
bitumen black
don't! that makes me think of roadkill!
redder than orange but not blood orange
ouch!   orange like a red-winged blackbird's wing
that sounds like a yank
i am a yank
looks like a bauhaus quill pen but it's probably trad from a remote community
indigenous communities don't do bauhaus   or art deco
sonia delaunay   the old busch-reisinger museum in cambridge   mass
on sabbatical i went to concerts there   the organist   e power biggs
biggsy!   they've relocated to a renzo piano building now
chicago art deco skyscrapers
don't forget new york's chrysler building
my uncle had a nile green chrysler
it says it's a fan
like a flying bird   two feathers on top & then a gap   the others below

says the feathers are stuck in beeswax
copies in the shop?
not a lot of market for hand-held fans
closet moths would eat the feathers   like felt   moths love felt
they could have the design reproduced to sell
    postcardsgreetingcardsplayingcards   silkscarvesshawlsakubrahatbands
    earringsjigsawsthrowcushions
show some fucking respect
not commercialise it?
preserve it
the shadows look like treescapes
check out the coffee in the cafe?

fat chair

Fat Chair (Fettstuhl) sculpture by Joseph Beuys, 1963
wood, fat and metal

why call me fat
i am lean from exhaustion
>my legs groan under this yellow load
>*vain travail hath wearied me so sore*

>>the burden on my lap
>>a thick wedge like parmesan
>>fat oozesseepsjigglesripples me
>>no place for the weary to sit

>>>that knotted wire   for hanging the wedge
>>>or severing it

beuys's pun:
>*stuhl* = chair = stool = shit
>the nation's tallow debt
>pushes against my back

>>>>during a crimean blizzard
>>>>beuys crashed a german fighter plane
>>>>tartar nomads rubbed animal fat on his wounds
>>>>wrapped him in felt   warmed & healed him

>>now he is the shaman
>>using fat & felt to heal a nation

>>>*in a net I seek to hold the wind*

Noli me tangere, for Caesar's I am

      for hitler's i am   says the big smelly cheese

          and wild for to hold

how many malnourished bodies did it take

how many exhausted stars of david

          to render fat

             no one can see without remembering

Freedom of Thought
after André Breton

André Breton in *The Magnetic Fields* of bachelorhood   *If You Please*

André Breton's marriage with *Earthlight* in the *Surrealist Manifesto*   *Soluble Fish*

André Breton with his *Legitimate Defense*   *Second Manifesto of Surrealism*
Slow Down   *Men at Work*

André   still married   but *Free Union*
                    'my wife with the hair of a wood fire'
                            i remember her woodfire hair

Immaculate Conception

André   wifeless   *Poetry's Misery* and other *Communicating Vessels*
The Automatic Message   *The White-Haired Revolver*

He marries again
Mad Love Trajectory of Dream at *The Starry Castle*
Break of Day   *Notes on Poetry*   *At the Black Washtub*

Breton's Surrealism   *Political Position of... Abridged Dictionary of ...*
What is ... ?

Fata Morgana   *Anthology of Black Humor*   *For an Independent Revolutionary Art*
Arcanum 17   briefly wifeless again

Marriage #3

Young Cherry Trees Secured against Hares   Four-Leaf Feral   Red-handed
Martinique: Snake Charmer   Magical Art   Free Rein   Poems 1919 – 48

Coffee table talk   *Situation of Surrealism between the two wars   Yves Tanguy*
Conversations   The Autobiography of Surrealism   numerous translations
and retreads

André Breton dies
Ascendant Sign   Cavalier Perspective   Breton   The Complete Works   tomes
1   2   3

marriage of convenience

a small painting of marquis lodovico's daughter
dorotea sent from mantua by courier   to be
inspected by her would-be spanish groom   he'll
check if her nonna's genes are tangled in the gonzago
laundry   (her younger sisters & their deformities
already packed off to convents)   despite cruel
allegations & medical examinations   sweet dorotea
frescoed to the wall   asserts her capacity to
strengthen alliances   & trade flesh to breed heirs
the spaniard accuses her of being a hunchback   &
weds the sister-in-law of the french king

amore of the moon

madonna of the maidenform bra
she hangs with parrot-wing angels playing lutes
sleep-deprived school girl madonna with her grandaddy
wakey babe with pianist's fingers
our lady of grace in her twenty-four carat halo
frowning at a beggar
her with the brat gobbling grapes
gesturing with *this is the church and this is the steeple* hands
her plucked eyebrows and birkenstocks
madonna of the crypt that leaks
now she' s breastfeeding in church
madonna of the dragon bones
her tiara of murano light bulbs
madonna who ate truman capote's venice—
a whole box of chocolates in one afternoon—
madonna outside the brothel
of one thousand seven hundred and thirty steps
when the moon's in the sky like a gold pizza pie
that's madonna

assembling a daughter

after *A Journey*, 2011-12, by Judith Wright
a sculpture in twelve figures
Sydney Biennale 2012, Ian Potter Centre

narrator: thirty years after the birth
an artist searches for materials
to build a baby daughter

she checks eBay   art auction catalogues
she remembers mummies at mona
a noh theatre exhibition somewhere

a halloween visit to a costume shop
theatrical wardrobes in storage
rags from a bank of the ganges

the nightmares of sepik river mothers
the dreams of disabled javanese youth
sales at poorhouses & asylums

give me your stained   your maimed
the ballerina mother is theatrical
grief takes dramatic forms

narrator: this child in the antique wheelchair
this child with broomstick legs
she should be able to wheel herself
her metal fingers hammered & nailed
her elbows articulated
she rests her madonna head against mellow wood

woman: like the wood of a cello

narrator: in the child's lap rests a school case
inside are patterns for simple shoes

woman: but
she'll never walk

narrator: the potential of girl twists back
over her shoulder   her gaze fixed

woman: one way or another
i keep my daughter alive

narrator: mumikin in a grey wig
pushes a tub with yellow wheels
dolly body crouches in a corner
dummy face   bulbous nose
sad sad eyes
a stripped down kid
too much exposed

woman: i ignore stares before i see them
i ignore jeers before i hear them

narrator: on her lap sits the spoonbill half-child

woman: i pin fresh flowers on top of her head

child: i'm a flower pot

woman: a head & torso is better than no child

child:	scared in a billycart without brakes
	my bamboo elbows out at angles
	knees out at angles
	shrieking
	how can i steer
	red wheels
	out of control
	my mum hoards
woman:	shoe lasts packed in cubby holes
	a canvas stretcher stamped thornleigh station
	masks for the back of the head
	ghosts of earworms
child:	some times i clutch her
	some times she clutches me
	some times i want her to let go
woman:	a window dressing mummy on a stand
child:	my ballet dress mum
woman:	lacking grace & waist but
child:	like a chess piece on a stand
woman:	it's so cold
child:	can i have a cuddle?
woman:	it wasn't my fault the doctors agreed

child: well it's not my fault!

woman: ten piano fingers &
              ten ballerina toes

child: like any other
              fingers & toes

woman: i can cope

child: a cuddle please?

woman: our life must

child: the show must

woman: go on

              i'm fine   really i'm fine

child: really

narrator: a red-headed school girlikin
              wheels giraffe body parts
              in a wicker pram

child: so embarrassing

narrator: the schoolgirl looks over the top of the pram
              she's big sister & this   this two-headed giraffe
              is not the baby she ordered
              she longed so long
              for a baby to kiss
              now her mouth is sealed

child: i don't have a big sister

narrator: the owlet sitting on the wooden kayak
                it must mean something?
                wisdom?   the mother
                with paw-print breasts rows
                with one paddle

woman: you want wisdom? i'm way too exhausted

narrator: & this glum staring child

woman: my bamboo & wooden burden

narrator: never a thought in its poor head

child: never a thought in my poor head

woman: masked undertakers
                who looked like drug dealers
                they stole the stretcher   they stole my baby

child: mum gave me a white glove to hold the cane

narrator: the pink ballerina
                from a european boutique
                wheels a purple tutu
                it'll never pas de deux

mother: to save her
                from the special school bus
                i pick my daughter up
                & hear myself scolding
                pull in your tongue

child: i try to be good

narrator: the girl's gloved hands hold her head on

woman: every day: humiliation
               we're all better off

child: mum carries ballet shoes on her back
               no kid to take to ballet lessons
               no kid to ride the rusty two-wheeler
               with the empty basket
               no kid to fill her ballet shoes
               no kid to fill her slender arms

child: mum pulls a rubber horse head
               over her own head

woman: thirty years i grieved
               before i searched for the place
               my daughter was buried

child: her torn trackies
               held up by jute

woman: i scull a zinc tub
               across a river
               a nest of yearning birds
               her baby grave

madonna of the peaches

after Petrina Hicks' print, *Bruised Peaches*, 2018, NGV, Melbourne

her immaculate skin hair lashes nails bra
dulux shades from the cold moon
paint card   even the wall looks drained
the pale virgin cradles ten bruised peaches
each an attempt in the conception lottery
no archangel clutches a lily
no messenger from god
take a light song & make it darker
madonna becomes stone   there will be no baby
barrenness offers some comfort
no need for a crucifixion

mary has a few questions for god

good morning

my name is gabriel & i'm calling on behalf of god
your name has been selected   can you spare just three minutes
i'd like to speak to the youngest female member
of the household   between the ages of thirteen & forty six
yourself?   seventeen?   excellent   may i call you mary?
fear not for your details mary   our privacy & security regulations ...
in a hurry?   excellent   fear not mary   i won't tell
your number has been randomly selected to receive
a unique spiritual gift simply by confirming a few details
your full name?   excellent   your date of birth?   fear not mary
your credit card number?   excellent mary   expiry date?
your CSN?   your pin?   now about your free gift
within three days mary   from our immaculate messenger

For best results

test two weeks after ovulation. Your pregnancy test choices include the classic dip and swim test and the midstream test. Easy to read results in two minutes brought to you by hCG, the pregnancy hormone. Alternatively, our number-of-weeks digital test comes with a conception indicator & clinically proven dual sensor: one line you *are not*, two lines you *are* pregnant. Five lines indicates the possibility of quintuplets. Free charts of Centrelink subsidies included. 97% accuracy. Add to cart? In cases of an unwanted positive, blow gabriel@gateofheaven.gov.au. Results will be displayed for twenty-four hours, allowing time for selfies with or without possible fathers. Big fat negative result? Use our assisted conception service. Customers who bought this product also bought Pregnancy & Breastfeeding Gold Capsules. Add to cart? Go directly to check-out. Free delivery.

git your high self

into this fuckin house now   ya slut
you're still my daughter   so stay away from joey's fuck truck
ya hear?   he's fuckin my age   older even
shaggin wagon fame is not okay
just coz lizzi got herself   you wanna too
like some film bitch   you hear me?
you & joey rent your own place   far from judaea east
hail yourself around   have a blessed sprog   move in
with lizzi's family   i don't fuckin care what mr gabriel said,
young lady   your father and i haven't slaved like pagans
for you to flaunt that belly in a bikini   all teachers are red
in the head   call yourself a virgin
before your shame shows   piss off to nazabeth heights
if you don't like it   see how you like going back—
—back to finish year eleven

mary has a few questions for god

thank you for calling god's chatline   please enter the ten
commandments which appear on the bottom left hand corner
& then press the hash key located on the bottom right   thank
you   this is the main menu: to establish a bequest, donate to the
usurers' benevolent fund, or increase tithes, press one   to
speak to the collector of unpaid taxes, press two   to support
projects placing putti on undeveloped ceilings, press three   to
return to the main menu press star   your prayers are important
to us   at the present time we are experiencing a high volume of
supplications   your number has been placed in a queue   at
present the wait is forty five minutes   did you know that
petitions for baptisms & marriages may be left on our website at
any time   go directly to www.god.com   we apologise for any
inconvenience   your number has moved higher in the queue
at present the wait is fifty five minutes   thank you for calling
god's chatline   your faith is important to us   to establish a
bequest, donate to the usurers' benevolent fund, or increase
tithes, press one   to speak to the collector of unpaid taxes,
press two   to support projects placing putti on undeveloped
ceilings, press three   to return to the main menu press star
your belief is important to us   did you know that through
prayer you can plead directly

hurry up please

after TS Eliot, *The Waste Land*, 'A Game of Chess'

when i heard god cuckolded joey
fair go   i said to mary myself   if you want joey back
you'll have to be extra virginal   get a fresh hymen
with that money he gave you to get your boobs done
he did   i was there   nip the babe in the bud mary
& git yourself *a nice set he said   i swear*   i'm not going halves
with any bloke he said   & neither should you i said   poor joey
listening to all gabe's lies   when all he wants is a good lay
& if you don't give it him, there's others will i said   oh is there
she said   then i'll know who to thank she said
& give me her pious look   no fun being a single mum
i said   & you sure can't boogie both at once
if joey scoots through   well no one'd blame him
you ought to be ashamed i said   giving god the nod
(and her only seventeen)   *i can't help it she said*
putting on her face   took the morning after pill too late,
the doctor said the pill would *bring it off*   six months gone she said
you are a proper fool i said   well if joey wants
to bury the bishop there it is i said   what you
git with god for *if you don't want* kiddies

muse to the rescue

he mentioned the old place with the stables
& from his lips she sketched the perfect studio

the one no real estate agent had conjured
& from his brushed up lips she drew

pretend i am climbing a grant & it's
arthur boyd's studio on the shoalhaven

in pencil she sketched the cows & flies
the perfect hillsides growing kellogg's corn flakes

& from his lips she needed joyous music
so she herself sang arthur's praises

though arthur was never his favourite artist
she juxtaposed the bluest skies

beside his bleached self-consciousness
a pot of golden coins is dangerous in dry tinder

more dangerous than turpsy rags
& from his arse she drew the perfect paintbrush

then arthur boyd's studio became his
to lie about & fall asleep & paint in

morandi's room

when the sky turns the colour of milk
he shifts an easel to capture the light
via fondazza   only one room
olive oil   ovaltine   so many bottles
he niggles a basket   it nudges a bowl
from the kitchen he fetches a funnel to study

in bologna smart artists don't study
the shades   the hues   the tones of milk
he coats the insides of jugs & bowls
catches transcendental light
he swirls white paint into the bottles
his sisters ignore the smells from his room

he tells the maid   do not enter my room
do not close catalogues open for study
do not dust the dust from my bottles
it's dust that renders them matt as milk
he's obsessed with games of shadow & light
arrogant vessels & humble bowls

the maid serves *brodo* in a chaste bowl
europa's in chaos outside his room
mussolini simmers in half light
buys two morandis to hang in his study
when the war ends   venice is top milk
the venice biennale   world in a bottle

a lemon squeezer—a break from bottles—
ribs & cones among the bowls
he skews their shadows   milks
fresh life from his crockery room-
mates   *natura morta* the only study
roma   milano   dada by daylight

a global depression   his pockets are light
the clock keeps ticking   so empty the bottles
the clock keeps on ticking   cold as his study
he approaches his dealer with a blue begging bowl
returns with seurats for his sisters' rooms
the kindness of kin   of dealers   of milk

politics is a distant room   etching's his study
his milky pastels   cream on a bottle
bowls overflow with ivory light

portrait

clutching his armani manbag   hadrian flees roma
on the steps of temple not yet constructed
maimed & mournful gypsies beg him for small change & changes

refugees try to sell him sun helmets   umbrellas   selfie-sticks
he condescends to buy a rose   his chariot grumbles past the city gate
up the autostrada to his villa near tivoli

he picks wild asparagus   carries the rose through cyclamen-stained
groves checking each tree trunk & column for shadows
along the canal past the fish pond where turtles swim in pairs

his favourite servant (the boy's cheekbones
too blunt   his chin a little sharp) swings open the bridge
to a moated island with three-key security

one key for the villa   one for the bar fridge
one for the safe within the fridge where he places
roman coins   passport   iPhone & a small likeness

thirteen ways of looking at a sunflower seed

after Wallace Stevens, and *Sunflower Seeds*, 2010, by Ai Weiwei,
White Rabbit Gallery

a treat in the mao years   some days
sunflower seeds were our only food
*
on the gallery floor   a mound of porcelain seeds
painted by villagers
visitors pass six precious seeds
hand to hand
*
in famine a man & a sunflower seed are one
are the artist   the people of jindezhen
& a porcelain seed also one
*
among twenty snowy mountains
cold fingers kneading clay
*
a fear pierced weiwei
on the gallery circuit— is the art
the making or the idea
*
in a crunch of *green light*
a half ton of sunflower seeds—
walk on them   hear them break
*
to stop seeds jumping into pockets
art guardians erected barriers
*
weiwei *was of three minds*
like a tree in which there are

one thousand six hundred
unemployed workers
*
why do you imagine gold
do you not see
the sunflower turning its head
*
we *did not know which to prefer*
the comfort of money
or the comfort of the full belly
our slipcast seeds for sale
or just after
*
small seeds in galleries—
we know the rhythms
of cross border translations
*
one hundred twenty thousand dollars
at sotheby's   many pockets filled
we follow our porcelain road
*
for sale on ChinaBuy—our sunflower seeds   direct
twenty five cents each plus one fifty postage
it was evening all afternoon on taobao

mr cook adjusts each cabbage

after William Delafield Cook's *Three Cabbages*, 1977, NGV, Melbourne

out of the dark
a trio of cabbages
on a quaker-simple table

a cezanne-tilt to the top
flattens the picture plane
sends blessings of light

cook has adjusted each brassica
negative spaces increase tension
heads two & three touch

the left cabbage
a pregnant belly   skin
stretched so tight it splits

the middle crucifer   vermeer's virgin
with the pearl earring
a scarf tight around her neck

rose petals wrap the flirtatious right
a peek-a-boo bunting unfurls
here I am   come here   go away

like magritte's lovers
eyes noses & mouths veiled
silent & still   their secrets safe

no one is here

after Lucy McRae's video, *The Institute of Isolation*, Ian Potter Gallery, NGV

the assistant she hired   a drone   hovers
over the art brut castle's cement walls

purple pavers   black door
white knob   formal gardens

an abandoned celadon greenhouse
decay edged in weathered copper

        she rides a suspended bicycle
        wheel rotations thump under the ceiling

        she races against herself
        there is no one here

        desolation the colour of pea soup
        giant pasta industrial tubes

                electrodes monitor stress
                record her physical needs

                the machines   the drone
                hungry for data

                what measurement can predict
                the effects of isolation

                one in ten who winter in antarctica suffer
                psychological problems

descending the cherry stairway
she's pale as her tailored wet-suit

        the crowns of defoliated trees
        a frozen canopy

        her body lies rigid on a raft
        the pounding noise intensifies

        the drone   like a companion animal
        watches her swimming alone

        a hexagonal pool of haunted water
        she circumnavigates the austerity of silence

parramatta road   annandale

after Edward Hopper's painting, *Early Sunday Morning*, 1930

a row of paired sash windows
       above shops
weary blinds, once white
       half-lowered
pairs of curtains dust-heavy
       behind dirty glass
two windows stare back
       depression-shame-black
one shop's awning pleated
       fancy as a church hat
(i imagine chapeaux on stands
       mannequins in frocks)
ready for the sun to radiate
       from the pavement
burn shopfronts
       bakelite brown

behind silent curtains the barber's wife
       remembers brake squeal
remembers the iceman's eyes following
       breasts
 the dry-cleaner's daughter
       before the baby

all day the barber's wife
       watches shadows
of fire hydrant & barber pole
       shrink toward noon
lengthen & rust at sundown

Corpus Viderum

in response to Ryan Walsh's performance at Central Park Phoenix, June 2022
*What would a cathedral dream of?** *

people slump on benches
lie pillowed on the floor

> *Viderum: an open data solution** *

may the powers of AI grant us
    thousands of thousand-year-old stained-glass windows
    sharded onto a trinity of screens
        a crucifixion of light
        dawning behind hanging panels
                a st john's spider of light

arches emerging & merging

        ghostly shapes of family
        villains' shadowed faces
        shades of apostles
        saints & biblical heroes

                banners of emerald & streams of blood
                edged in lead

may the powers of AI grant us
    thousands of thousand-year-old notes of sacred choralwork
        *Viderunt omnes, a Gregorian chant** *
        mashed into a gothic sound track

salve regina mater misericordiae
vita dulcedo et spes nostra salve

*viderunt: third person plural perfect active indicative of video***

salve regina mater misericordiae
vita dulcedo et spes nostra salve

no one sleeps

the time went quicker than i expected   my grandson says
the faces   i liked the faces

2

o my chevaliers

danes   germans & english cross the atlantic
homeless snow falls on ellis island
falls on herricks   flecks & chevaliers
immigration clerks change nissen
to nason   then, later it's mason
put your arse on *la table*   said aunt fanny
aunt fanny learns english   plays her ace on the table
french & swiss neighbours marry in brooklyn
danish cabinetry is valued in brooklyn
a new york job for a gold engraver
platinum letters   embossed on gold watches
DFC my monogram mother
(thank goodness her first name didn't start with K)
they cross the hudson to live in new jersey
julie's french laundry truck gives me its name
 the melting pot adds frasers to frazees
my daughter & her husband choose chevalier
divorce means single with kids & grandkids
seven assorted australian flavours
they study german & japanese   french & hungarian
sydney knight flights   i'm a tourist in italy

postcard

the photographer waits behind his tripod
in the shadow of the statue
snaps me squinting   wrinkling my nose
the stench of rubber   boiling hot dogs
red skins stretching   bursting into yellow scum
why would he take this photo no one will buy

give me your tired   your poor
we climb step after step inside her hot body
inside her head the stairs narrow
her huddled masses hot & cramped
yearn to breathe free   she's crowned
with flyblown windows   i belch
the hot dog smell   my sister & cousins
hog the air   she lifts her lamp

at horn & hardart's automat
in boxes behind windows edged silver
apple pie & six nickel cake iced pink
i slot coins into the glass door
touch the hot knob of a food box
my stomach churns the whole statue of liberty
into one postcard no one gave me for my birthday
i really really wanted that postcard
yellow bubbles rise   i throw up
i am scum   i am wretched refuse

cape breton island

they nibble their way along a sour path
blue terrain & little cash
She had been getting hungrier for a lifetime

insects with dinner   weather reports paper over
the austerity of boulders
the severity of frost

then moonlight   silver as the teeth
of sleeping bags   can newlyweds zip together
in a 6 x 6 tent with a centre pole?

she is the wildest thing
the next wildest thing is the jasmine
he is wild as foxed wallpaper

i am dying of hunger she said

Driving Route 1 outside Boston, 22 November 1963

leave work early   drive north along the sea
    frantic news flashes
        static
        what can you expect from an old V-dub radio?

            an open topped limo in a political parade

    a motorcade guard is shot   Texas city guards
            stunned

        the governor   shot

        & him   shot

                the sun caught between Icarus's feet
                  plunges through fences

        they rush by ambulance
            the hour another's   each struggles alone
            death on the operating table

        the assassination of the president

    & then the roaring
        the autumn rain stopped

acceptance of blood on flesh
on Jackie's face   nylons
pink wool
I want them to see what they have done to Jack

deafening clouds
the tear-blind in cars
(not just me)
stopped on verges
nowhere near Texas
a gummy box of tissues

The Book Depository office window
the shot

& then another shock

& much much later

another parade   his funeral
echoing Lincoln's cortege

Jackie calls this Camelot?

Jeoffry

after *Jubilate Agno* by Christopher Smart

I testify I was one of only four women going *in quest of food*
by teaching in the boys' high school. Consider this: in my first class dwelt
thirteen Geoffreys, Jeoffrys or Jeffreys, nine Garys or Garrys, four Gavins
and two Garths. *The Lord's poor* included Keith, Kevin, Kelvin and Trevor
of the tribe of Tiger. Sir Charles Kingsford Smith's propeller hung
on the library wall keeping *the Lord's watch in the night*
against the adversary. When the photo of Sir Charles *looks up*
for his instructions I ask him to spin me out of Sydney Technical High
over the parking lot, past the science and maths teachers' Fords and Holdens,
their bumper stickers spruiking Billy Graham's long gone revival crusade.
It appeared that the entire Maths/Science Faculty had accepted
English cats as *the best in Europe.* It was 1968.
The glory of god was in the air. As were drugs.

On April Fool's Day as we car-pooled past the newsagency
Ray (Commerce) said, Look at that sign, 'LBJ quits.'
'Naahh,' I said *with a mixture of gravity and waggery,*
'Probably cigarettes. Not the presidency, surely.' I'd picked up 'surely'
trying to *spraggle upon waggle* at Sydney Uni.

If I'd known the tune I would have danced
Plath's *love set you going like a fat gold watch.*
I sailed down the library corridor in the psychedelic spinnaker
I wore on odd days, just as a Third Form student
whistled, *Yummy yummy yummy i got love in my tummy.*
I certainly had. *By stroking ... I* had *found out electricity.*

'No, only seven months. Two to go.' *Afraid of detection* I lied
to Principal Brown, who, by July, with *the passing quickness
of his attention*, still had no idea who I was.
Every family had one cat at least in the bag. But, *catching the cork
and tossing it again*, what to name the sproglet if it were a boy?

Plan B

after Vivienne Plumb, *The alternative plan*

Plan A: find man sympathetic to children but who loves me best of all. *Plan B:* become pregnant. *Plan C:* surf web re older mothers & childbirth. *Plan D:* establish relationship, difficult enough without a child. *Plan E:* buy lingerie, stay single & childfree. *Plan F:* push borrowed labradoodle pup around block in borrowed $1,200 pram. *Plan G:* stay single & have baby that doesn't bite. *Plan H:* search web for sperm donor without tatts. *Plan I:* have one-night stand with only gym bloke not on steroids. *Plan J:* prick condoms with sterile needle. *Plan K:* second-night stand with same gym bloke (despite 'roids). *Plan L:* separate finding partner from acquiring child. *Plan M:* search web re twins by artificial insemination. *Plan N:* time travel to 15th century Florentine orphanage with Kathmandu carry pack. *Plan O:* move to Italy, *this plan requires* proficiency in Italian & a grant. *Plan P: think of another plan. Plan Q:* search web re overseas adoption agencies with sympathetic international agreements *(finance dependent). Plan R:* arrange wealthy patron, superior sperm & gravy baster without telling therapist. *Plan S:* observe o/s adoptees' picnic in skanky suburb. *Plan T:* terminate contact with sperm donor & surrogate agencies. *Plan U:* visit a single mum's chat room disguised as Leila the foetus. *Plan V:* join kidnapping chat room. *Plan W:* become novice in Our Lady Queen of Procreation Convent *Plan X:* pray for visitation from male angel with no active addictions & grand sperm count. *Plan Y:* Search web re Renaissance names. *Plan Z: Change nothing.*

embroidery

with a crocheted lasso around a single
button above his carotid artery
i tethered him   i cross-
stitched ties & cabled jumpers
of possession   french-knotted the orifices
in our intimate garments   darned escape
hatches in the toes of his socks
zipped his sense of domesticity to mine
i buttonholed my affirming echo
to the clone in the mirror
i bribed araldītē   goddess
of matrimony   to cement him to my side
tighter than any chain stitch
then reader   i left him

leaving

dear pay phone used to call real estate agents
  agents of change
dear fearful decision slow baked in ovens & kilns
dear leave him now or you'll be a bitter old woman
dear lists of the thousand scariest things with kids
   i will live in the house of poverty forever
dear house i did & did not want to leave
dear garden where i learned to grow
   allergic to native plants
dear doctor who said you live with a husband & two kids
   can't one of them use long-handled secateurs?
dear husband who went on sabbatical alone
   thinking there is a train going one way, and a train
   going the other way, each at different and variable speeds
dear teenager who looked forward to talking for one hour to his dad
dear teenager who had been put in a box & someone was sitting on it
dear you must miss him terribly when i didn't
   we clung to the outside edges of the shrunken bed
   i took sad train whistles to bed in my studio
dear husband with whom i divvied up our cargo
   did you wonder later as i did
   why you chose the italian & spice island cookbooks
   & i chose three volumes of bertrand russell?
   didn't we know?
dear disappearing table of tiles i made and raku fired
   I was not who I am now
dear husband who loaned our year's mortgage payments
   to his sister & went overseas without telling
dear husband who then told me to pay his income tax
dear was it fair for me to leave a good person

        the hand that removed the ring
        the hand that signed
        is not my hand now
dear McCavity cat
dear teenagers who stuck by me
i was so happy you lived with me
dear parents   ashamed of my failure
dear elderly aunt   i sent sins of omission
the waiting space
i was happy to sleep on a mattress on the floor
dear daiso pen i write with now   juicy & full of life

The lunar experience

after 'The cinematic experience' by Vivienne Plumb

If the man in the moon *takes his hat off, he is either being polite or he means to stay.* If our lady of the moon *takes her shoes off, it's either sex* or blisters. A crescent moon *will indicate a* shallow *storyline,* or *something is about to happen. Like* cutting toenails. Filmy curtains billowing on a balcony *always means sex.* The appearance of an eclipse means it will get dark fast. *But worse.* Clouds streaking across a bad moon rising *indicate either* bad *sex* or a storm at sea. Or possibly bad sex on deck during a storm at sea. *The removal of clothes* in a moon shadow means someone sat on a green cheese sandwich, or sex with a green cheese sandwich. Yellow, blue or silvery moonlight in Vermont even in June or August does not mean you will see the one you love. A harvest or paper moon ditto. Seeing the lunatic you love *is never that straightforward.* Consuming moonshine *ditto, but double all of the above.*

this is the poem the town passes through

this poem passes through laundry on balconies
terrace house verandas chained to bicycles
letter boxes averse to junk mail

people in this town worry about the carbon paw prints
of dogs   about old ladies in brittle black demanding
'what day is it   what day, what day'

this poem passes through a park groomed by ibises
the bandstand a bird cage aching with emptiness
the letters above the library spell biblioteca

this poem passes over bridal dress showrooms,
flower-girl and tuxedo-boy salons
bomboniera   galleries of gift automobiles

this is the poem where a woman tells a barista
'i was in labour but who can deliver
in a two hour zone   i caught the bus'

the streets of this town are padded with cafes
pastaorpizzapastaorpizzapastaorpizza
this is a poem celebrating parmigiano reggiano

'tim tam & milo   cool names for a dog
on the bus   media students chat up lecturers
everyone buys gelato at bar italia

soccer is celebrated all night on norton street
but *this is the poem the town passes through*
during *la festa* when everyone is working

this poem lives under the flight path
this is a poem celebrating the italianate
if there were a *campanile* we'd climb to the top

but there is only the town hall where rats
infiltrated the ranks   this hall remembers
old labour councillors who didn't vote

with the liberals   now the mayor can be
any colour but green   a phase the town
is passing through   this is a green poem

branding

venice   where every green & white   & red & white   & blue & orange
& yellow & blue pole   moonlights as an extra in films
where the floral tribute on the deck of a gondola & its red velvet seats
have been sited as far away as cockatoo island in sydney harbour
during a biennale   where a gondolier's shirt (minus
the muscles beneath) hosts a dedicated kiosk
at st marco's square   where wingéd lions roar
on tea towels & magnetise ten thousand fridges
where the terrazzo floor of the accademia (& the room i share
in a mansion) has been reincarnated in vinyl
where every madonna, babe & angel has spawned chandeliers
of christmas cards   & every murano bead has its own website
& every sunrise   sunset   clothesline & pigeon stars on a postcard
& every bridge has its own technicolour month on a calendar
& even the monk's tonsure has been appropriated
by a nike-wearing cappuccino-sipping tourist from kansas

next year in venice

monolingual queen of the sea.
it's the dusk at punta della dogana i'm after
golden globes & domes in purple mist
i'll employ a remedial language expert
who won't talk to anyone carrying a phrase book
his job   to take this tourist
for a velvet gondola ride through
tenses most commonly used

conversation is table tennis
& i'm unable to return a volley
never land agreement in the proper court
i can't discuss caravaggio's
artichoke incident in any dialect
i walk the walks   order meals brokenly
every refugee speaks better italian than i do

santa chiara da montefalco, umbria

c1268-1308

to the hermitage door i follow my sister
at six years old i take the habit
a keyhole exact & i am the key
sharp as a harp string
no hold or cold word stills my ardour
afternoons exacting   god-exalting
the future faced without falter
each altar   a promise

after epiphany i fast
a vision of jesus
          where art thou going?
his cross too heavy to carry alone
for my offer of help
he plants wood in my heart
a crucifix like a thorn
& plants a strange tree
in the convent garden

rescuing treasure in firenze

smell the bells   hear the smoke   a cart's on fire
out the window   crackling   near the cappella
a wheel hits a pig eating fishbones
you grab a map   go out in pajamas

knock back a caffé at a bar full of smoke
the dog's bark contagious
a horse shies & whinnies
under a tower you bubble-wrap paintings

like pig's bones the crunching of relics
your arms ache from lifting   baroque
frames are heavy   the dog barks again
marble or bronze   what those statues get up to

you drag library books
down michelangelo's stairs
if you see alighieri welcome him back
on a night like tonight all is forgiven

marino marini donates rider & mare
you copy mosaics   paste them on domes
you colour in sandbags   drag venus
& cupid   a shed of tired shepherds

florentine bridges fall down like fair ladies
hitler's favourite the only one standing
if it's not barbarians   it's mussolini or allies
it's napoleon   an earthquake   the pope

a singed bat's wing frizzles your hair
the soles of your boots moulder & smelt
you wrap your cold hands around a bold brandy
save fra lippo lippi   winks one of the brothers

watch out   brush the spark off your shoulder
wake up   climb the ladder   your night is important
click & save   shut down   back to sleep
it's four in the morning   have a nice stay

gelato at london street   enmore

an afternoon hot enough to wilt all green things
the air con's cactus
bar italia has been invaded by greece

after balsamic strawberry fieldwork
we search for greensleeveless gelato
bypassing messina pistachio
our cow and the moon prayer answered:
mandorla affogatto cones

back home duolingo whistles   duolingo knocks
my accent untuned   due to TPG/telstra
inaction again   (they had the sense not to charge)
affondare: to sink   affogare: to drown

too hot to worry about coal seam gas
remembered instead arnica
the black & blue flavours of childhood
bee stings   blackberry scratches   lemonade
thunder rumbled & we ran like chickens

another step away

in homage to Frank O'Hara

a fix of toby's estate coffee on the footpath.
baird has sold the education department
& another heritage building:
archival storage boxes re-labelled 'wine glasses'

past the museum of sydney — martin sharp's
tunnel of love — rows of ancestral totems
names of the dead as mournful
as first people circular breathing down at the quay

the art of war is showing at the gallipoli club
the bar girl winks   her cubes
languorously agitating   a man slumps on the door
of a soon-to-open restaurant

around the corner gulls stir-fry the air
someone in a sari hurries
towards the noodles of bridge street
the sun is hot   a silver statue stifles a sneeze

outside customs house   buskers on unicycles
juggle flames & gimme signs
at wharf six   captain cook
directs travellers to the bondi explorer

the infirm struggle to board 'the radiance of the sea'
ferries turn beneath a jacaranda sky
the harbour arch crawls with climbers
in search of a mountain

outside the mca rows of green tufts implanted
on bald ground   a baby magpie is fed
shredded lettuce   a man in a hoodie competes
with ibises for poly-boxes in bins

in the rocks five maseratis & two passengers
dressed in ribbons & lavender fur
halt all traffic without permission:
the importance of filming their music video

yellow helmets protect labourers from talkback radio
it's my lunch hour, so i go

kill care

care & maintenance of your architect-designed registered trademark   use
the grab-it sweeper to keep the lawn leafless   or vacuum to remove dirt
astroturf does not require hydration   the underground solar heating is
guaranteed to be passive   keep electric outlets hidden under floor boards
the fridge & freezer are concealed beneath the glass cook top   composition
of clutter dependent upon proximity of children   lifetime guarantee
may be employed for white doona covers on bunk beds   flexible storage
facility for adolescents   sterilisation is not necessary   avoid contact with
skin & eyes   touching with finger may damage bulb   please test on an
inconspicuous spot   if consummated contact poisons information centre
storage duration required may vary   polish with silver cloth to give all-
over protection from infants   adolescents showering without supervision
is not recommended   tighten trigger before aiming gooseneck nozzle at
youth   pull-down storage compartment sleeps twelve   brand name surf
at the door   beach within easy walk not to be used in conjunction with
use of house   add two capfuls to half a bucket (four litres) warm water
thorough rinsing of feet is monitored   enjoy

what are you competing against

four pairs of magpies chortle
septuagenarian in gym gear alert
j slams the car door   turns up abcfm
these are quality of life years
often they play *morning mood* on this time slot
but never strauss's *four last songs*

in the spin room she pedals
with lycra wolves of the imagination
up and down rpms of hills with *zorba the greek*

she follows the pack into gym one
where john brack's pencil-sharp
models crunch   & botero's pneumatic models
lift weights   she pictures larry rivers' mom-in-law
tensing glutes for a hip flexor stretch
she observes male artists observing women
nothing changes   everything changes
you don't live longer   you just die fitter

press up   sit up   *she & dripping sweat*
usually do not appear in the same sentence
but today is thursday   exercise or die
she compares her old sneakers to other's
lolly-coloured footwear   everyone genuflects
like planks   then genuflects again
to the gleaming machine grinding toby's beans

laptopland

your passport is out of depth   keep a code in a quadruplicate place
drop it into a box or a cloud   to renew your password enter
answers only you know the questions to   family secrets
are good   her net is not shark-proofed   but she's immunised against
exotic viruses   answers must refer to eleven local characters & contain
at least three equations   not part of your date of birth   phone number
or area code   if all else fails   change your holiday destination
the model of your favourite pet   the name of your dad's
maiden uncle   click to request the protection of a firewall
then enter your date of expiry   turnover & key in
the three digit tattoo on your back   umm   bluebirds
#tweet your one hundred forty character epitaph now

waiting with dignity

into one hostage story anne carson crams
a python named robert   zombie slaves
chinese tourists in greece   putin
extract of puffer fish   the urge to piss
the british museum   how boring torture can be
& lapsang oolong falling off the counter
what an exciting life anne carson must lead
while cranky pants waits at home for telstra & tpg

out front corellas watch magpies
peck a pink praying mantis
perhaps a female insect has cannibalised
her partner while sexting
or perhaps it's just a drone like the kids
down the road got for christmas
how can cranky pants identify things
if she can't google without wifi?

she respects a company that doesn't try
to sell her products while she waits to complain
& hates charities that attach pleas to their receipts
& what about slashing arts funding but finding
eighteen mil to hype creativity & start-ups?
her local barbeque shop closing down sale
lasted for thirty years   & moss river bedding
needs nembutal the peaceful pill
there should be a statute of limitations
on liquidation & demise

wifi is restored for a while   the insect drone
has been eaten or flown & there are enough
corella & magpie feathers to fill a pillow slip
for robert the blue tongued lizard
cranky pants ignores the urge to piss
googles to find out if the pope
will see the people from ballarat
& puts on the kettle

Stained

after F Scott Fitzgerald's *The Great Gatsby*

This incredible guy, Jay Gatsby, the best, has a friend from Goldman Sachs, another truly great guy, Mr Wolfshiem. Wolfshiem wears the best cufflinks. Human teeth. Everybody looks at them, honestly, everybody. I described them to Ivanka for her accessory line. I promised Flynn, ex-National Security guy, a pair. Golden handshake. Not bad after twenty-four days on the job. I gave Sean Spicer a pair when he quit. The Mooch got his. I even promised Putin a pair but sh-h-h-h, very hush hush, okay? Everyone will want these cufflinks! So I said to Ivanka, she's a great great gal, isn't she? Very, very important to me. So said to her, a little business *gonnegation*. Get the molars anywhere you can. The real deal, right? Don't let anyone use whitener on them. I will say this, I have great, great sources. I really do.

trappings

i'm not unzipping my skin   if a fastener had been at the back of my
neck i'd have felt it   in the days when i was desperate to try
everything   i'd have been outta here & into a tiger pelt   actually that's
not true   i've have unzipped a tiny bit   maybe slipped one arm out
examined what passion looked like   wiggled the fingers   the left arm
the way blood is taken from my left   less harm if there's a mistake
like starting at the choc bunny's feet & nibbling up to its head   just last
week my daughter told me she ate the head first so the footless bunny
wouldn't topple   my old boyfriend bit off the head & feet   saved the
furry bit   what kind of person does that   i drag my new skin off the
hook at the back of the door   examine those handles on the shoulders
wriggle into the cover of *the female eunuch*   handles for someone to
pick you up & carry you through the glass ceiling to a world without
mirrors   zippety do dah   where five-inch heels don't exist & your suit
is fuzzy yellow pjs   built in feet with non-slip treads   a trap door at
the back   the thick hide of a writer who has exposed herself in public

shades

in the intensive room
coated nineteen shades of white
to anesthetise agitation & fear
his soul is ready to levitate

i remember trader vic nights
in tropical new york
when i was a chinese gooseberry virgin
dipped in sour cream & muscovado
skewered on bamboo
rum & gardenias
knots of little fruit at play
interrupted floating love

all too soon nineteen shades
of worn umbrella
the smell of naphthalene
the slow dusk drawing down blinds

the 3am

it wasn't much   i layered me down   i couldn't feel
a featherless hope   it wasn't down to sleep
restless sleep   denying sleep
ignoring it   there wasn't much he didn't drink
there wasn't much i couldn't find   myself
i wasn't down   his dying   it wasn't much
pray for it?   my guilt   his sodden soul?
i couldn't distance myself   i didn't drink
there wasn't much i didn't name that night
(still clinging to   still singing old apologies)   i never pray
no words to shroud   no time for blame
there wasn't much that i could do   if i should die
i wouldn't wake   there wasn't much that i could feel
my soul to take   i couldn't breathe   it wasn't much
there wasn't time for mends   amends   amen

don't fence me in

martinis are in the dry goods aisle
let me be by myself
hammocks & inclinators
mobility scooters
the checkout chick googles facilities
dutiful daughters home help
rehabilitation   assisted care
aged care   nursing homes
she directs me to the rust belt aisle
palliate *till i lose my senses*
nooses & nembutal   the escape button
in wet goods   beyond blue tissues

help wicked witch of the north north west!
just let me wander way out yonder
dorothy was the name
of my nonagenarian aunt as well as mom
two dots   no dash   dot dot dotty dot dot
send me off forever
but is that scarecrow kansas
under starry skies above?
then i'm in the vortex of a tornado
help dorothy! tin men! medical wizards!

rainy   stay at home   five visitors max

a fortune-teller's neon sign
that glowed a painted light into the street
— Bianca Stone, 'I Saw the Devil with his Needlework'

after seeing out the old prosecco with fresh
food from people delivering seven days a week
(the unexpected success of my peach tarte tatin
followed by celestial seasonings' sleepytime tea)
just after dusk i drove abandoned streets
saw a pandemic of empty pubs and supermarkets
saw the best minds of my generation addicted
to airline timetables   fretting cancelled holidays
cancelled restaurant bookings
the supernatural darkness of cold-water flats floating
across the tops of cities contemplating jazz
cities off-limits in a new world/aged world
outliving its options

back home   beneath apartment verandas
pavement lights bloomed from cylindrical stalks
sandstone's golden promise
an avenue of palm trees   magnolias in blossom
odes on the windows of the skull

incandescent hope teetered on balconies
pulsed   LED lights strung out
rooms pooled scarlet   violet   aqua
at nine   illegal fireworks at the corner
a starry dynamo in the machinery of night
dancing silhouettes *their brains   bared*
cheered to heaven from the loggias

i clapped like i had clapped alone
for local medical heroes   cheered
at midnight for protean miracles
too personal to mention
a confetti cloud   champagne spray
cascades of summer   the pent up *hollow-eyed*
jiggled   red zinger tea
angels staggering on tenement roofs illuminated

Notes

Artemisia Gentilischi Plays Wordle: Court record quotation *from Artemisia Gentileschi* by Jonathan Jones, Lives of the Artists series, Lawrence King Publishing, London, 2020, p.35

fat chair: Sir Thomas Wyatt, *Whoso List to Hunt I know where is an Hind* Biographical information plus Beuys' pun: stuhl (chair) = stuhl (shit/stool) from Columbia University Press blog, www.cupblog.org/2012/03/20, sighted 25.10.21

Corpus Viderum: * www.giartent.com/XX/Unknown/275439683368326/ Phoenix
** Wikionary

cape breton island: italicised lines from D H Lawrence's *The Rainbow*, 1915

leaving: italicised lines and inspiration for this poem from Kerrin McCadden's *Epistle: Leaving*

this is the poem the town passes through: lines in italics from *The Poem*, Craig Sherbourne

shades: *nineteen shades of white* and *knots of little fruit* from Amy Gerstler, 'The Underworld', *slow dusk drawing down of blinds* from Wilfred Owen, 'Anthem for Doomed Youth'

don't fence me in: italicised lyrics by Robert Fletcher and Cole Porter

rainy   stay at home   five visitors max: italicised lines from Allen Ginsberg's *Howl*

Acknowledgements

Many of the poems in this book have been published, performed or recorded, sometimes in slightly different versions.

Many thanks to:
Australian Book Review, Australian Poetry Anthology, Australian Poetry Journal, Contemporary Australian Feminist Poetry, Best Australian Poems, Flashing the Square, Flashing the Square Federation Square Screen, *Cordite, Gargouille, Meanjin, Rabbit, Southerly, The Weekend Australian, WRIT Poetry Review.*

assembling a daughter was performed at Story Fest, Customs House, Sydney with funding provided to Spineless Wonders/Little Fictions from the Literature Board of the Australia Council.

thirteen ways of looking at a sunflower seed was awarded the Rhonda Jankovic Literary Award, 2016, second prize.

Many thanks and much gratitude to David Musgrave, Morgan Arnett and Ross Gillett at Puncher & Wattmann and Gary Pedler at Scampe

About the Author

Julie Chevalier came to Sydney from Cambridge, Massachusetts in 1965. She is the author of the short story collection, *Permission to Lie* (Spineless Wonders, 2011) and the poetry collection *Linen Tough as History* (Puncher & Wattmann, 2012). *Darger: his girls* (Puncher & Wattmann, 2012) won the 2011 Alec Bolton Prize for best unpublished manuscript and was short-listed for the WA Premier's Award for Poetry. Her writing is frequently published and performed.